PROVINCIAL BUSES IN COLOUR: 1960s

B. S. Watson

Ian Allan
PUBLISHING

Front cover: Seen parked in the sunshine outside Eastbourne Corporation's depot on 7 June 1963 is No 16, an immaculate 1946 Leyland Titan PD1 with an East Lancs body, and one of the first postwar buses to be placed in service by this operator. It had been converted into open-top form at the end of the 1961 summer season and was back in service the following year. The street lamps provide a nice period touch and the advertised one-hour coastal ride for 1s 6d (7½p) now looks to be excellent value.

Back cover: The AEC Regent III was part of the manufacturer's postwar range, and the design was popular with both crews and passengers. The Model O961 featured a 9.6-litre engine, chromium-plated radiator surround, fluid flywheel, air-operated pre-selector gearbox and air brakes. A variant known as the 9612A had a clutch and four-speed sliding-mesh gearbox, and an example is seen in Newcastle Corporation No 321. Dating from 1950, it was fitted with a locally-built Northern Coach Builders 56-seat body that was to be one of the last built. The yellow and cream livery positively gleams in the spring sunshine on 15 April 1963, contrasting with the more sombre colour scheme of the Tyneside Leyland Titan parked behind.

Title page: This contrast in body design was captured at Blenheim Palace on 9 June 1963. On the left is United Counties No 473, a 1953 Bristol LS6B with a 41-seat Eastern Coach Works dual-purpose body. On the right is a vehicle from the highly individualistic Midland Red fleet — No 4240, a 1954 underfloor-engined C3 coach fitted with a 37-seat centre-entrance Willowbrook body. The wording on the destination screen of the latter vehicle displays a touch of originality, whilst the United Counties vehicle relies on the more prosaic 'Excursion'.

First published 2001

ISBN 0 7110 2792 7

© Ian Allan Publishing Ltd 2001

Published by Ian Allan Publishing

an imprint of Ian Allan Publishing Ltd, Hersham, Surrey KT12 4RG.
Printed by Ian Allan Printing Ltd, Hersham, Surrey KT12 4RG.

Code: 0105/B2

Introduction

With the benefit of hindsight it can be seen that the 1960s were to prove to be a watershed in the bus scene in Great Britain, although most enthusiasts who lived through that period probably didn't realise it at the time.

Perhaps we were all too busy enjoying the tremendous variety of vehicle types that were still to be seen in revenue-earning service — prewar vehicles, wartime utilities, petrol-engined single-deckers — and all this alongside the introduction of such exciting new designs as the Leyland Atlantean, the Daimler Fleetline and the Bedford VAL.

The trolleybus was also still a force to be reckoned with, for at the start of the decade there were 22 systems in operation, and extensions were still to be made to some of them. There was also considerable variety in operators, for at the time there were still 97 municipal fleets, in addition to British Transport Commission companies, the British Electric Traction group and a multitude of independents, all running a vital network of stage carriage services in an era when private car ownership was nowhere near as widespread as it is nowadays.

The next 10 to 15 years were to bring about tremendous changes that were to alter irrevocably the face of bus operation: the introduction of the bus grant scheme, the annihilation of the trolleybus, the arrival on the scene of the National Bus Company, the formation of the first Passenger Transport Executives (PTEs), and local government re-organisation. The outcome of all this upheaval was that fleets were merged and local identities and liveries became lost.

We were also to see the rapid decline of crew-operated buses (with the notable exception of London Transport). This change was assisted in no small part by the introduction of rear-engined chassis designs, and later by the repercussions of the bus grant scheme, which effectively signed the death warrant for the traditional half-cab, open-rear-platform double-decker.

Changes on the operator front were not the only ones to occur. Notwithstanding the inevitable loss of trolleybus manufacturers, it is noteworthy that, with the exception of Dennis, all the other chassis manufacturers featured in this volume have now ceased to exist. Forty years ago this would have seemed impossible. At that time the bus industry was virtually 'home-grown', with little or no European influence. Who could have foreseen the upheavals that were just over the horizon?

For a youthful enthusiast the 1960s were a marvellous time, and any journey across the country was one of wonder, revealing an apparently infinite variety and individuality amongst operators. It should be borne in mind that the magazine *Buses Illustrated* was a 'must' for all enthusiasts —

but it was printed in monochrome, and actually to see buses in all their colourful glory was usually a pleasant surprise, although sometimes not what you'd previously imagined!

The overall feeling was that the situation would remain static in the well-ordered 1960s. Although new vehicles were being delivered, withdrawals appeared insignificant, and there were always other interesting vehicles still on the scene. When changes did start to occur, however, they came thick and fast — older vehicles disappeared, trolleybus systems vanished with indecent haste, and old-established operators and liveries were swept away. The new looks and new images that were beginning to affect all aspects of life finally began to make an impact on the transport scene, and suddenly it was too late to photograph those favourite buses that had never previously been captured, because 'they were always there'. So often they had been overlooked in favour of something 'more interesting', or 'less mundane'.

A short section at the end of the book deals with contractors' buses, used to convey workers from central collection points to construction sites. Not only were these operated by companies for the exclusive use of their own workers, but some companies were actually established to provide this service for third parties. Some interesting vehicles could be seen enjoying this form of 'after-life', often operating far from their original haunts, although they didn't usually last long on this sort of work. In any case, the increase in car ownership and the arrival on the scene of minibuses were both factors that helped bring about the demise of these often-colourful vehicles.

Right: Bedford's six-wheel, twin-steer VAL chassis created some excitement when it was announced in 1962. It could take bodywork up to the (then) legal maximum overall length of 36ft, and originally was powered by the Leyland O.400 diesel engine, driving through a five-speed overdrive top gearbox. Later it was fitted with Bedford's 466cu in diesel, which was retained until production ceased in 1972. The 16in-diameter wheels allowed a low floor-height, and, with power steering, the vehicle had a surprisingly good turning circle. It was claimed that the three-axle layout allowed a more even load-spread and that there was greater safety in the event of a front-wheel puncture.

Wilfreda Luxury Coaches Ltd of Ranskill, Nottinghamshire, soon obtained this 'cherished' registration number for a Duple Vega Major-bodied VAL, seen at Newark Show on 9 May 1964. The wording on the destination blind is worthy of note.

With one exception, all the illustrations in this book were taken by the author in 1963/4, so they present a snapshot in time of an era that we shall never see again. It is felt that they are of particular interest, not just for the main subject matter, but for the street scenes in general — the fashions, the other vehicles in the background, the period advertisements, the street furniture, the overall lack of other road traffic (and litter!). They were all taken with a period Kodak 35mm camera, on colour-slide film. None of the subject matter was posed; the scenes were simply captured as they happened, in all weathers and lighting conditions, and purely for personal enjoyment. Certainly there was no thought that at some future date they would be presented to a wider audience in a book such as this.

Hopefully, all these glimpses of the past will bring back memories and provide nostalgia for those who, like the writer, nurtured or further developed their love of transport in the 1960s. If the reader derives as much pleasure from studying the contents as the author had in making the selection, then the effort will have been worthwhile.

Barry S. Watson ACIB
January 2001

Left: Following the success with BTC operators of the Bristol Lodekka, which gave the low height advantage of a lowbridge bus without use of the unpopular sunken side gangway arrangement on the upper deck, AEC made a decision to build a similar vehicle for sale on the open market. The design and development work was carried out by Crossley, part of the AEC empire, at Stockport, and the Bridgemaster, as it was to be known, was first exhibited on that firm's stand at the 1956 Commercial Motor Show, badged as a Crossley. With bodywork by Park Royal, it was of integral construction, with sub-frames front and rear and coil-sprung suspension, although air springs were later used at the rear, and became standard from 1958. The model was produced until 1963, by which time only 180 had been built.

Registered in 1957, 76 MME was a 72-seat demonstrator, seen here on hire to Nottingham City Transport. In 1958 it was acquired by Barton Transport, becoming No 805 in that fleet. *Author's collection*

Right: In 1941, at the height of World War 2, the Ministry of Supply instructed Guy Motors to manufacture a wartime version of its Arab double-decker. The first one came off the production line the following year, and the design evolved into the Arab II, which remained available until 1946, by which time approximately 2,500 had been built in total.
A surprisingly large number of these vehicles soldiered on into the early 1960s, notwithstanding that they had originally been produced as a stop-gap to meet wartime shortages.

Barton Transport No 432 was an example, fitted with a low-height 55-seat Duple body. As with most such survivors, it had been modified by the fitting of upholstered seats, but the overall character and 'feel' of the utility vehicle remained. Standing next to it, at Nottingham's Broad Marsh bus station on 17 May 1963, is No 874 from the same fleet, a 1960 Bedford SB1 with a 41-seat Plaxton coach body, adapted for stage-carriage use. The rear of a Strachans-bodied Guy Arab can be seen on the far right, showing the neat platform door and emergency exit arrangement.

Left: The vehicle parking area adjacent to Nottingham's Huntingdon Street bus station, used both by local stage-carriage vehicles and those on long-distance services, was for many years a favourite haunt of bus photographers. This scene, photographed on 20 July 1963, shows, from left to right, Barton Transport No 722, one of the company's Leyland BTS/1 rebuilds with a 39-seat Plaxton body, and Guy Arab No 432 with a 55-seat Duple utility body; next is East Yorkshire Motor Services No 740, an immaculate Harrington-bodied Leyland Leopard, named *Beverley Star*, while just visible on the far right is a recently-delivered Bedford VAS1 with a 29-seat Duple Bella Vista body, No 84 in the fleet of Mulley's Motorways of Ixworth, Suffolk.

Right: Within months of the end of World War 2, Leyland launched its new double-deck bus chassis. The PD1, with a 7.4-litre diesel engine, four-speed constant-mesh gearbox and vacuum-assisted brakes, proved to be just the reliable and economical vehicle that operators required. With minor improvements, leading to the PD1A variant, it remained available until 1951, even after the introduction of its successor, the PD2. Leyland offered complete vehicles, the five-bay body being an updated version of the prewar design, with simple but classic lines.

An example of the all-Leyland vehicle was DJF 344, dating from 1946 and supplied new to Leicester City Transport as No 243. It passed to Barton Transport in 1960, and became No 877. Here it is parked up between duties in Nottingham on 12 June 1963, sporting the joint Barton/Robin Hood fleetname, the latter company having been acquired by Barton in 1961.

In 1950 a change in the British Construction & Use Regulations allowed single-deck buses to be built up to 30ft in length on two axles. Barton Transport, an operator with a reputation for being very resourceful, decided to produce its own vehicles to the new dimension, with units taken from various Leyland Lion, Tiger and Titan chassis. Barton even built its own bodywork for some of these vehicles, although bodywork was also provided by Beccols, Duple, Massey, Plaxton and Strachans.

No 726 was one of these rebuilds, designated BTS/1, with a body both designed and built by Barton, dating from 1954. It is seen standing at Nottingham's Broad Marsh bus station on 17 May 1963.

A unique vehicle was Barton 861, a Dennis Loline II chassis fitted with a Northern Counties 68-seat lowbridge body. The body, fitted to a low-height chassis, combined to give a vehicle with the remarkably low overall height of 12ft 5½ in — nearly 12in lower than a standard lowbridge double-decker. It was exhibited on the bodybuilder's stand at the 1960 Earl's Court Commercial Motor Show, entering service in 1961 and remaining in use until 1976. Parked in Mount Street, Nottingham, on 26 August 1963, it presented a very modern aspect with its curved glass windscreen and upper-deck front windows. It had originally been fitted with a Cave-Browne-Cave heating and ventilation system, but this had been removed by the time the photograph was taken.

Above: Yeates of Loughborough was not renowned for producing restrained body styles on its single-deck range, and Barton Transport No 949 was a fairly typical example. In this instance the operator's paint scheme had been married to the styling to good effect, producing a striking vehicle. Dating from 1962, this Europa body was mounted on a 36ft-long AEC Reliance chassis, the resultant vehicle being seen on stage-carriage work in Nottingham on 29 April 1963. Yeates was acquired by Duple the same year.

Right: Guy Motors' Arab III model had a bonnet line that was approximately 4in lower than its predecessor's, giving the driver better visibility. This early-1950s example, owned by Birkenhead Transport and fitted with a Gardner 6LW engine, had an East Lancs body that featured that builder's distinctive ventilators, fitted above the lower-deck side windows. It was standing at Birkenhead Woodside on 8 October 1963 in company with several other buses from the Merseyside operator's fleet, and was to remain in passenger service until the end of 1968, after which it was retained for driver-training duties.

Left: The vast former LMS/GWR station building at Woodside, Birkenhead, forms an unmistakable backdrop to this picture. Sandwiched between Birkenhead town centre and the Mersey ferry terminal for Liverpool, the bus station was a busy place in the morning and afternoon peaks, although this view, taken on 8 October 1963, captured the scene in quieter mood.

Birkenhead's fleet was always smartly maintained and No 78, a Leyland PD2/40 fitted with a Leyland O.600 engine, synchromesh gearbox and vacuum brakes, was a good ambassador. Fitted with a 65-seat Massey body, it had been delivered earlier that year. Parked behind is a Leyland PD2/12 dating from 1954.

Despite the fairly recent introduction of rear-engined double-deck chassis by both Leyland and Daimler, many operators still preferred traditional half-cab vehicles, although circumstances were soon to change the overall scene. Birkenhead Transport would later become part of Merseyside PTE.

Below: When considering transport in Blackpool it is the trams that invariably spring to mind, but this famous Lancashire resort had, for many years, run an interesting bus fleet serving the needs of its outlying suburbs. A large proportion of the fleet carried bodies to Blackpool's own design, most of which were built by locally-based H. V. Burlingham Ltd, taken over by Duple in 1960 and becoming Duple Motor Bodies (Northern) Ltd.

A batch of 100 Leyland PD2/5 Titans delivered in 1949/50 was fitted with air brakes in place of the standard vacuum brakes of the PD2/3; the full-fronted, centre-entrance bodywork seated 52. No 251 waits near the time clock at the Cornwall Place, Marton, terminus on 9 October 1963, ready to return to Central station on route 16B.

Another seaside-resort operator that favoured full-fronted double-deck bus bodies was Bournemouth. Dating from 1939, No 21 (FEL 204) was one of 16 Leyland TD5s delivered with 7.9-litre versions of the manufacturer's Mark III petrol engine. In fact this operator was Leyland's largest customer for the petrol-engined option, although these were later replaced by 8.6-litre oil engines. The Weymann dual-staircase body, with rear entrance and front exit, seated 48 and boasted a sunroof. A tired-looking No 21 was still fitted with semaphore trafficators when parked at The Triangle on 4 June 1963.

This is how some of Bournemouth Corporation's 1939 Leyland TD5s were to end their days — in open-top form, on scenic tours along the seafront and to the resort's famous chines. When the roofs were removed the opportunity was also taken to dispense with the front staircase, thus increasing the seating capacity of the Weymann body by 10, to 58. No 11 was rebuilt thus in 1960, and was photographed at Bournemouth Pier on 3 June 1963 with a modest passenger load, all of whom had opted for the lower saloon rather than the exposed upper deck.

Below: Following trials in 1933 with four different trolleybus models from three manufacturers, Bournemouth Corporation placed bulk orders with Sunbeam for the latter's six-wheel MS2 model, and after three years had a total of 103 in service. In 1958 three of these were converted to open-top format for use on circular tours of the town. On 4 June 1963, ALJ 986 waits for the traffic to clear before pulling out from the Pier Head turning circle. Only the informed would be aware that this vehicle was nearly 30 years old, having been built in the boom years of UK trolleybus construction. Although the day was fine and sunny, none of the passengers has taken the opportunity to sample the fresh air available on the top deck.

Right: If any of the passengers had ventured onto the top deck this is the sight that would have greeted them — varnished wooden seats, the steel framework supporting the two trolleypoles, and an uninterrupted view over the holidaymaking crowds and traffic. Note the white-coated policemen controlling the pedestrian crossing, and the period vehicles on the road — all now but a memory.

MIND YOUR HEAD

No 202
NO STANDING

Above: Bournemouth Square was the heart of the transport system, with routes radiating from it. Trolleybus No 249 is seen leaving by way of Richmond Hill, *en route* for Winton and Ensbury Park on 4 June 1963. The hill provided a stiff climb for any vehicle but was no problem for trolleybuses, with their smooth and powerful acceleration.

No 249, a BUT 9641T with a Weymann body, was one of 24 delivered in 1950 which were to be the only BUTs to be bought new by Bournemouth, where Sunbeam was the preferred manufacturer. It was originally numbered 215, but had been renumbered in the late 1950s.

Top right: T. Canham & Sons (Services) Ltd of Whittlesey, Cambridgeshire, operated stage-carriage services into Peterborough in competition with Eastern Counties. On 24 August 1963 the duplicate service was being covered by LMG 184, a 1939 Leyland Lion LT8 with the manufacturer's own 39-seat body, and powered by a Leyland petrol engine. New to Eastbourne Corporation as No 15, and registered JK 8421, it passed to the War Department during World War 2. In 1945 it was acquired by

Valliant Direct Coaches Ltd, at which time it was re-registered. Seen at Peterborough bus station, it was in its last year of operation. Canham's continued in business for a further 20 years, services ending on 21 October 1983.

Right: Leyland's TS7 model was introduced in early 1935 and was built until 1937, differing from its predecessor, the TS6, in having a vacuum-hydraulic brake system. DJE 554 was a 1936 example, acquired by Canham's of Whittlesey with the business of Pywell at nearby Thorney. It was actually a hybrid, the chassis having been registered to East Yorkshire as CKH 249; it was later fitted with a 1947 Duple body previously on a 1932 Maidstone & District Leyland Tiger TS2 (KR 8384). It was used by Canham's from 1954, and is pictured at Peterborough bus station on 24 August 1963, its last year in service.

The vehicle on the left belonged to Booth & Fisher, an independent on the outskirts of Sheffield, which was bought out by South Yorkshire PTE in 1976.

18

Coventry Transport favoured local chassis and body manufacturers for its bus fleet, and this Daimler CVA6 with a Metro-Cammell 60-seat body is a good example. One of 96 delivered in the late 1940s, it was to remain in service until the end of 1964. The body is a standard Metro-Cammell design, with styling that borrowed heavily from prewar design practice. Maroon and cream was a popular colour combination with municipal operators, enlivened on a dull March day in 1964, in the centre of Coventry, by the gleam from a chromium-plated radiator surround.

Derby Corporation used an unusual shade of green as part of its fleet colour scheme, not seen at its best in this wet scene in June 1963. Normal practice was for both the upper- and lower-deck panels to be painted green, but on No 112 an attempt has been made to lighten the overall effect through the use of cream in substitution on the upper panels. One of five delivered in 1951, this Crossley DD42/8A was fitted with an 8ft-wide, 56-seat Brush body. The '8A' in the chassis designation indicated the fitting of improved suspension and a radial rear engine mounting. This scene, full of period interest, is at Derby Midland station.

Left: The Derby trolleybus system opened in 1932, and a compact route network was developed, with extensions being opened until 1958. Sadly, it fell foul of the anti-trolleybus sentiment of the early 1960s, and operations ceased on 9 September 1967.

No 180 was a Sunbeam W4 (wartime, four-wheel) chassis, one of 15 delivered at the end of World War 2. The utility body was built by Park Royal to a standard 56-seat layout. It was photographed in the Market Place on 29 June 1963, the dull light having prompted the driver to turn on the interior lights. The side advert provides an appropriate touch, whilst the names of the two banks in the background are now, like the trolleybus, only a memory.

Below: Doncaster's first trolleybus ran in 1928, and a number of quite short routes were established, all of which ran to and from the town centre, there being no cross-town services. By the time that this picture was taken, on 14 September 1963, the small system had exactly three months left to operate.

CDT 637 was a wartime Karrier W — new in service in 1945 and originally fitted with a Park Royal body — that had been rebodied by Roe in the 1950s. It is seen here on the circular Race Course route, vehicles running round the circle in the opposite direction having 'Hyde Park' on the destination blind. The latter route had been abandoned on 10 December 1961, whilst the Race Course route survived until 13 October 1963. After the end of the system a successful rebodying exercise was carried out by transferring 20 trolleybus bodies onto diesel bus chassis for further service.

W. Gash & Sons Ltd of Newark, Nottinghamshire, started business in 1919, and the fleet was well known for its excellent condition. An example is DD6 (KNN 959), a 1949 Daimler CVD6 with a 56-seat Roberts body with a platform door. It stands in Newark bus station on 7 September 1963, a miserable and very wet day, waiting for its crew before departing on the company's trunk route to Nottingham. To travel on such a vehicle was always a pleasurable experience, as the smoothness of the ride was rarely equalled. Gash's continued in business until 1988 when it was taken over by Yorkshire Traction.

During the early 1960s it was still possible to find prewar buses in revenue-earning service, and one such example was this Leyland Tiger TS7, owned by Gilbert's of Tunbridge Wells in Kent. Its Stockport registration (JA 5514) suggests original ownership by North Western Road Car Co, and indeed it was new to that operator in 1935/6. The handsome Harrington body, with stepped waist-rail, dated from 1939. Vehicles such as this would have been a regular sight on the Manchester-London coach service in the early postwar years. Owned by Gilbert's since 1953, it was found in Tunbridge Wells on 19 October 1963.

Above: Loading at the Hants & Dorset bus station in Bournemouth on 4 June 1963, in preparation for a run to Sandbanks, is No 1128, a Bristol K5G with Eastern Coach Works body, delivered new in 1947. Subsequently converted into an open-topper, at which time a full front was fitted by the operator, it made a very smart vehicle, although it had not been deemed necessary to fit flashing trafficators. Some of the lady passengers on the top deck have their headscarves in place, obviously being aware of the stiff breeze that will be encountered on the journey.

Above right: The entrance to Poole Harbour forms a natural obstacle to any direct road route from Bournemouth to Swanage, the only alternative being a lengthy detour through Wareham. The problem was overcome by the provision of a ferry, in the form of a chain-guided floating bridge, at Sandbanks, and this was utilised by Hants & Dorset on its direct route (7) between the two resorts. No 697, a 1951 Bristol LWL6B, is seen just starting the descent of the ferry ramp on 2 August 1964; its Eastern Coach Works body has been modified with angled, cut-away, rear panels to give sufficient clearance on these ramps. This bus was to remain in service until 1967.

Below: Henry Hulley, of Derwent Garage, Baslow, operates a number of stage-carriage services in the Derbyshire Peak District. Photographed in Chesterfield on 5 August 1963 was an interesting second-hand acquisition in the shape of LHA 358, a BMMO S9 dating from 1949. Numbered 3358 when it ran for its builder, the Birmingham & Midland Motor Omnibus Co ('Midland Red'), this underfloor-engined machine was one of 100 with 40-seat Brush bodywork, later converted by Roe to a 44-seat layout. The small glass panel on the front, below the windscreen, reading 'Service', would have read 'Midland' in the vehicle's BMMO days

Left: In 1964 Lincolnshire Road Car had some unusually-modified Bedford OB coaches on its Skegness seafront service — the door and the nearside glazing of the Duple body had been removed to enable passengers to benefit from the famously bracing air of this East Coast resort. (The offside windows remained in place.) ONO 88, dating from 1949, had been acquired from Eastern National in 1958, and was to remain in service for a few more years as 'Road Car' No 1002.

Right: During the early 1950s bus traffic on rural routes began to decline, whilst costs rose. There was, obviously, a demand for a modern, economical vehicle for use in rural areas, and to meet this need Bristol introduced its SC model in 1954. It was of integral construction, with Eastern Coach Works bodywork, and was fitted with the economical Gardner 4LK engine, mounted vertically at the front of the chassis, driving the rear axle through a five-speed overdrive gearbox. Offered in both bus and coach form, it was bought by only a handful of operators, and production ended in 1961.

The Lincolnshire Road Car example seen here, No 2603, was one of a batch of 16 dating from 1956/7, its coach body seating 33. It was being used on an excursion to Stapleford Park, Leicestershire, on 18 August 1963.

The Maidstone trolleybus system opened in 1928. The route to Barming, on which the depot was situated, was the first to be converted from tramcar operation. So well were the new vehicles received that the route to Loose was converted in 1930, the terminus being situated at the junction of Old Loose Hill and Linton Road, where No 66 was to be found on 7 June 1963.

This was a 1946 Sunbeam W, with BTH electrical equipment, and bodywork by Northern Coach Builders. The red telephone box and the old-fashioned signpost provide a nice period touch to this idyllic scene, as do the tiny street lights using ordinary electric lamps, which would certainly not be considered acceptable on today's busier roads.

Pictured in the centre of Maidstone, on the route to Loose, on 7 June 1963, was No 85, a 1948 Sunbeam W with BTH electrical equipment and a Weymann 56-seat body. It had been delivered new to Hastings Tramways, a subsidiary of Maidstone & District since 1935, which was absorbed totally by the latter company in 1957. No 85 was one of five obtained by Maidstone when the Hastings system closed in 1959, and looked very smart in its livery of golden ochre and cream. The Maidstone system was to last until 15 April 1967.

Daimler's wartime double-decker chassis was offered with engines by Daimler, AEC or Gardner. The AEC engine was free-revving, and this factor, coupled with the pre-selective gearbox, which allowed for easier gear selection, enabled quite brisk acceleration to be achieved.

An example of the AEC-engined variant was Maidstone & District DH47

(HKE 283), a 1944/5 CWA6 which, in common with the operator's other utility buses, had been rebodied by Weymann in the early 1950s. Standing in Maidstone bus station on 7 June 1963, and wearing an advert for a famous Kent brewery, it awaits its departure time before running southwest from Maidstone to Chart Sutton. Its appearance belied its years.

Maidstone bus station in June 1963 provides the setting for two Maidstone & District Bristol K6As, representing what was the company's standard double-decker until 1950. Delivered during the war with utility bodies, both later received new bodies by Weymann to that builder's postwar standard, but incorporating detail changes to suit the operator's requirements. At the same time they also received PV2 radiators, and in this form were to outlast some postwar examples. HKE 241 was to survive for a further three years before being withdrawn due to a low-bridge accident.

Left: The Manchester trolleybus system peaked at approximately 150 vehicles, but was a shadow of the city's impressive tramway system which had needed 900 trams. Some tramway routes had been operated jointly with Ashton-under-Lyne, and this joint working was set to continue when trolleybuses were introduced by Manchester in 1938 (Ashton was already running them).

Two BUT 9612T vehicles, one from each system, were waiting together in Stalybridge on 10 October 1963. Loading in front is Manchester No 1324 (ONE 724), dating from the mid-1950s and fitted with a 60-seat Burlingham body, and one of 62 that were to be the last delivered to this system. The other vehicle is Ashton No 83 (YTE 822), dating from 1956 and one of eight that, once again, were to be the last to be taken into stock. The bodywork on this one was by Bond, built at Wythenshawe. Both systems closed at the end of 1966.

Below: Providing a network of services to the north of Nottingham was a trio of companies that had been part of the old Midland Counties Electric Supply Co — the Midland General Omnibus Co (MGO), the Nottinghamshire & Derbyshire Traction Co and the Mansfield District Traction Co. The first two operators used an attractive shade of blue and cream as their fleet liveries, and an example from the MGO fleet is seen at Nottingham's Mount Street bus station on 9 May 1963. No 107 was a wartime Guy Arab II that had been rebodied by Eastern Coach Works in the early 1950s, and was ready to provide an afternoon short working on the B1 route to Heanor. This immaculate vehicle lasted until the early months of 1966, when it was sold for breaking.

Left: The AEC Regent II was the manufacturer's first postwar model, announced in 1945. It was a re-introduction of the prewar Regent, fitted with the 7.58-litre diesel engine (type A173, known as the '7.7'), a four-speed 'crash' gearbox and triple-servo-type vacuum brakes. As the war had only just ended, allocation of these vehicles to operators was controlled by the Government. Approximately 700 had been supplied by the time production was phased out towards the end of 1947.

Seen here is No 122 in the Midland General fleet, dating from 1947 and fitted with a Weymann body. The complete lack of advertisements and the permanently-fitted starting handle are outstanding features of this smartly-turned-out bus. This operator was one of a minority that favoured the combined use of letters and numbers in its route-numbering system, this example being used on a short working of the A1 service to Langley Mill, from Nottingham, on 23 August 1963.

Above: The Bedford OB was introduced in August 1939, and fewer than 100 were built before manufacture had to cease, owing to the outbreak of World War 2 and Vauxhall Motors' involvement in war production. The model was re-introduced in October 1945 and continued until October 1950, by which time more than 12,500 had been built. The standard bodywork was the Duple Vista, but at one stage the demand was so great that Duple could not keep pace with it, and other bodybuilders stepped in. The Duple was definitely the favourite with operators, however, and sales of its bodywork on the OB easily exceeded those of any other builder.

Two Duple-bodied models are seen on 30 May 1964 a short distance from the entrance to the National Tramway Museum at Crich in Derbyshire. In the ownership of 'My Lady' Coaches, they were due to work the service to nearby Ripley.

Newcastle was well known for its six-wheel trolleybuses, but it did own a small proportion of four-wheelers, one of which was seen at the terminus of route 32 at Wallsend Boundary on 15 April 1963. No 475 was one of a number of Sunbeam F4s delivered in 1948/9, using Metro-Vick electrical equipment and fitted with Metro-Cammell 56-seat bodies. These had been ordered as Karriers, but were delivered with Sunbeam badges, following the sale of the Rootes Group's trolleybus interests to Brockhouse. The Newcastle system would finally be abandoned in October 1966.

The smoke-blackened walls along the side of Neville Street, near Newcastle's Central station, provide a stark backdrop to the bright yellow and cream of the city's No 528, a 1948/9 Sunbeam S7. The locally-built Northern Coach Builders body was 7ft 6in wide and seated 70. This scene was captured on a cold spring morning in April 1963.

Left: The late-lamented North Western Road Car Co, of Stockport, was dismembered in 1972 and is now but a memory. Its stage-carriage services were split between Crosville, Trent and a short-lived entity that was part of SELNEC. Its coaching interests, whilst retaining the name, became part of National Travel. At one time its Bristol single-deckers were a familiar part of the scene in the north midlands and the North West, and one of these was parked at the rear of the bus station at Matlock, where the company had a depot, on 5 August 1963. No 207, dating from the late 1940s, had a Weymann 35-seat body and was to be one of the last of its batch to remain in service. It only had a little while longer to work for North Western, subsequently passing to Sir Alfred McAlpine for use as a staff bus.

Below left: Alexander's Y-type body was introduced in 1961 and has come to be regarded as something of a design classic. It is certainly much favoured by enthusiasts, and it is hard to believe that the original design is now 40 years old. North Western had only recently taken delivery of these examples when seen parked at London's Victoria Coach Station on 6 May

1963. Nos 958 and 954 were mounted on Leyland Leopard PSU3/3RT chassis, on a wheelbase of 18ft 6in, and were fitted with Eaton two-speed axles to give better performance on the company's long-distance express services.

Below: When introduced in 1929 the AEC Regal was a completely new forward-control chassis, built as a single-deck version of the Regent. Part of a new model range, it had been designed largely by the legendary G. J. Rackham, AEC's Chief Engineer, who had previously been responsible for Leyland's Titan and Tiger range.

The example seen here dates from 1937 and was bodied by Cravens of Sheffield. It had started life as Nottingham City Transport No 75, later being renumbered 275 and 779, before entering the ancillary fleet as No 801 in the late 1950s. It then became an employees' canteen, and is seen serving refreshments at the Trent Bridge trolleybus terminus on 11 May 1963.

Above: Services to Nottingham's vast Clifton Estate, lying to the south of the city, were provided jointly by Nottingham City Transport, South Notts and West Bridgford, and required the use of low-height double-deckers. No 73, a Northern Counties-bodied Daimler Fleetline seen at Broad Marsh on 28 April 1964, had entered service with Nottingham City Transport only that year, and looked immaculate without any advertisements. It was one of a batch of 31 and was the only one with a B-suffix registration number, the others being 72 RTO etc.

Right: Utility trolleybuses made available to operators during World War 2 were promoted as Sunbeam-Karrier W — an example of 'badge engineering' which followed the closure of Karrier's Huddersfield factory and the subsequent transfer of production to the Wolverhampton works of Sunbeam. The 'W' type was produced until 1948, by which time 474 had been built. Nottingham had a fleet of just under 40 utilities, some of which, with their original bodies, continued to give good service until 1965.

No 460, a Karrier, seen in Carrington Street on 13 May 1963, had a Roe body which, whilst built to wartime specification, carries vestiges of Roe's traditional, arched roof design. A Roberts-bodied AEC Regent III waits at the stop behind, working a route to Beeston.

Left: Problems can arise on the best-run systems, and in Nottingham on 21 May 1963 trolleybus No 471, a Park Royal-bodied Karrier W, had lost one of its trolleyheads and become immobilised. No 460, another Karrier W but with a Roe body, bound for Wilford on route 40, edges carefully past with guidance from 471's driver. This view gives a chance to compare the utility trolleybus bodies of two major bodybuilders.

Below: Nottingham City Transport's routes 43 and 44 traversed the city centre and were heavily worked, being just the sort of routes that were ideal for trolleybus operation. They were the province of the 7ft 6in-wide BUT 9641T with 70-seat Brush body, of which 77 were delivered in 1951/2. No new trolleys were bought by Nottingham after 1952, unlike some systems, but they were to survive as long as most networks. Here we see No 546, on 11 July 1964, entering the terminus of the 43 route at Bulwell Market. Route 44 continued past this point to terminate at Bulwell Hall Estate. The 43 was converted to motor-bus operation on 1 April 1965, the conversion of the 44 route following two months later.

Left: Bristol's K-type was first produced in July 1937, and production would continue in various forms for 20 years. With the introduction in 1950 of the KSW variant, Eastern Coach Works developed a handsome 4¼-bay body, an example of which is shown here. The Nottinghamshire & Derbyshire Traction Co had operated an interurban trolleybus system from 1932 to 1953, and this vehicle was one of 15 that were purchased as trolleybus replacements when the system closed. No 303, a KSW6G model, was photographed at Mount Street, Nottingham, on 29 April 1963.

Above: In common with many other coastal-based operators, Portsmouth found it expedient to extend the working life of some older vehicles by converting them into open-toppers, for use on scenic and seafront routes. No 5, a 1935 Leyland TD4 with an English Electric 50-seat body, poses in front of some early-1960s architecture at Clarence Pier, Southsea, on 5 June 1963. The conductor leans on the nearside headlamp in characteristic pose, awaiting departure time for Hayling Ferry.

Above: Portsmouth's trolleybus system provided comprehensive coverage of the peninsula upon which both the city and Southsea are situated. This scene at Portsmouth Dockyard is hard to date, with no cars or helpful advertisements, but records reveal the photograph was taken on 5 June 1963.

The trolleybus on the left, bound for Eastney, is an AEC 661T with a Cravens body — one of a number delivered in 1936/7. To the right is No 307, a BUT 9611T with a 52-seat Burlingham body delivered in the early 1950s. The Portsmouth system, inaugurated in 1934, had only a few more weeks to run, the last day of operation being 27 July 1963.

Right: One of Portsmouth's last batch of 15 trolleybuses, a BUT 9611T with English Electric equipment and a Burlingham body, is seen turning onto the seafront out of Clarendon Road on 5 June 1963. The livery of burgundy with white relief, gold lining and a grey roof had a distinctly prewar appearance, accentuated by the large fleetnumber numerals and the driver's white-topped cap. Abandonment of route 5, which was to be the city's last trolleybus route, took place only 7½ weeks after this photograph was taken. The lack of other traffic is noteworthy by today's standards.

49

Above: The Gosport & Fareham Omnibus Co, or 'Provincial', as it was more popularly known, ran quite a large number of prewar AEC Regents in the early 1960s. DOR 921, No 47 in the fleet, dated from 1939, and was fitted with a classic Park Royal body. SCG 623 was a 1957 Guy Arab IV with bodywork by Reading of Portsmouth. Both vehicles were in excellent condition when seen at Gosport on 5 June 1963, and were a fitting tribute to the company. Sadly, this long-lived operator passed to Hants & Dorset, an NBC company, on 1 January 1970, but its memory is not forgotten.

Right: Already 27 years old when photographed at Gosport on 5 June 1963, Provincial's No 35 belies its true age, certainly by condition, although the narrow, swept-back, teak-framed bodywork by Park Royal could only date from the 1930s. The radiator blind provides a nice period touch. This vehicle entered service in 1936 and was not withdrawn until 1967.

Above: The Gosport & Fareham Omnibus Co was one of those individualistic organisations that helped make the enthusiast's life just that bit more interesting. Starting out in 1872 as a horse-tram operator, and moving on to electric trams and charabancs, it became in the fullness of time the largest independent stage-carriage operator in southern Hampshire.

This scene, in the sparse surroundings of Gosport bus station on 5 June 1963, helps to illustrate this charismatic appeal. From left to right can be seen: FCR 198, a late-1940s Guy Arab III with a Park Royal body, acquired from Southampton in 1962; DAA 845, a 1939 AEC Regent I with a Park Royal body; CG 9609, a 1934 AEC Regal 4 with a 1957 Reading body (one of eight conversions undertaken 1957-62); and DOR 921, a 1939 AEC Regent I, again with a Park Royal body.

Above right: A superb line-up of Crossleys, seen at Reading on 8 June 1963. Reading Corporation had 12 of these (chassis type DD42/8), with the chassis manufacturer's own lowbridge bodywork, seating 52. Built to a width of 8ft and delivered in 1950, they were the first vehicles in the fleet to be fitted with semaphore trafficators, still in evidence in this photograph.

Below: Trolleybuses first appeared in Reading in 1936, the first route, between Caversham and Whitley, opening on 18 July. The network expanded steadily, with some route extensions being made in the postwar years. Seen at the Northumberland Avenue terminus on 8 June 1963 are two BUT 9611Ts with English Electric equipment and Park Royal 59-seat bodywork. Nos 140 and 151 were from a batch of 20 delivered in 1949, some of which were to remain in service until the end of the system on 3 November 1968.

Reading Corporation No 186, a Sunbeam F4A, was only two years old when seen on 8 June 1963, on the reverser at Whitley Wood. This vehicle, one of the final 12 to be bought by Reading, had a 68-seat Burlingham front-entrance body, the last such bodies to be built by the Blackpool-based company. The Whitley Wood extension was to be the last made to the network (on 14 January 1963), and two years later the abandonment scheme started, the system closing altogether on 3 November 1968. Five of these vehicles were later sold to Teesside, where they were to run for a few more years.

Bristol was part of the Tilling group, and at one time many operators favoured this chassis manufacturer for their fleets. However, the Tilling group was nationalised in 1947, and a stipulation was that both Bristol and bodybuilder Eastern Coach Works would be allowed to supply only nationalised operators, although existing orders were to be honoured.

Rotherham's bus fleet was 100% Bristol until 1949, and here we see EET 574, a 1948 K6B with a 56-seat East Lancs body. The vehicle looked pristine when seen in damp and drab surroundings at Rotherham on 1 September 1963, and was to remain in service until the early months of 1966.

Above: Rotherham was the fourth trolleybus system to start operating in Britain, and for many years operated a fast fleet of single-deck vehicles. In the 1950s a rebodying scheme commenced, and Roe 70-seat, six-bay, double-deck bodies were given to much of the fleet.

No 33 is a 1949/50 Daimler CTE6, originally numbered 93. It was photographed at the Kimberworth terminus on 1 September 1963, on a route that was to last until 1965, the year that the system closed. A tight turning-circle such as this always produced a high degree of tyre-scrub on the rear bogie wheels.

Right: Manchester's Victoria bus station, with the cathedral in the background, provides the setting for Salford City Transport No 372, a 1950 Daimler CVG6 with a Metro-Cammell 54-seat body. This was one of Salford's first 8ft-wide deliveries; to help the bus-washing-plant crews identify these wider vehicles, they were fitted with a small red dome mounted between the front upper deck windows. Two other unusual features of these buses were the frame for the front destination blind winding handles, and a shortened radiator shell, fitted to minimise accident damage. No 372 was photographed on 10 October 1963.

Left: As a result of the LNER and LMS railway companies' obtaining bus-operating powers in 1928, bus services in Sheffield and its environs were controlled by a Joint Omnibus Committee. The 'A' fleet worked within the city boundary, the 'B' fleet (jointly owned by the Corporation and the railway companies' successor, British Railways) served adjacent districts, and the 'C' fleet comprised railway-owned buses and coaches that were operated, for practicality, by the Corporation.

No 1328, from the 'B' fleet, is a late-1959 AEC Regent V with a 69-seat Roe body. The Regent V was introduced in 1954, continuing in production until 1968, and was available with a conventional radiator or, as here, with a concealed radiator and wide bonnet. Sheffield's livery was a bold

statement for a heavily industrialised steel-manufacturing city, but it was always well kept. The scene is Pond Street on 7 April 1963, on what is now the site of Sheffield Transport Interchange.

Below: Looking slightly aggressive as it stands in Nottingham's Broad Marsh bus station is RN 8639, a Leyland TD5 with postwar Alexander body, No 72 in the South Notts fleet. Formerly Ribble No 2073, it was acquired by its new owner early in 1961.

Another ex-Ribble machine, No 73 (CCK 651), a Leyland PD2/3 with 8ft-wide Brush body, stands on the right of the picture. This view was taken on 13 May 1963; the whole site has since been completely redeveloped.

South Notts started running services in 1926 between Nottingham and Loughborough, its route network expanding within that area and also, much later, including a service run jointly with Nottingham City Transport and West Bridgford UDC to Nottingham's Clifton Estate. In fact, the company always had stage services as its main activity and, interestingly, Barton Transport had a half-share in the business for many years.

Pausing outside the depot on its journey to Loughborough on 14 July 1963 is No 80, a Leyland Titan PD3/4 delivered the previous year and fitted with a Northern Counties 65-seat front-entrance body.

Right: On 14 April 1963 South Shields' Dean Road depot was a transport enthusiast's paradise, with motor buses, trolleybuses, and tram track still in its cobbled forecourt, although the last tram had run in 1946. The left-hand bus is No 136, a 1946 Crossley DD42/3 with a Crossley body, whilst next to it is No 149, a 1951 Guy Arab III with Gardner 6LW engine and Roe body. No 249 is a 1947 Karrier W with Metro-Vick electrical equipment and Roe bodywork. This is the sort of scene that can nowadays only be recreated at a working museum.

Below right: The South Shields trolleybus system was one of contrasts — on the one hand the industrialised Tyne Dock area, and on the other the seaside atmosphere of the Pier Head and Marsden Grotto. This photograph was taken at the latter, a coastal terminus, set high above the North Sea which can be seen in the background. The turning circle, at the end of a half-mile route extension, was opened on 22 July 1939, but it had only a few more weeks left to operate when this vehicle was seen on 14 April 1963. Sea air in such an exposed place was not kind to traction poles and overhead wiring, and the route enjoyed only sparse traffic out of season. No 253 was a 1947 Karrier W with a Northern Coach Builders body.

61

Passing under a low railway bridge on 14 April 1963 is South Shields No 209 (BDJ 81), a 1951 Sunbeam F4 trolleybus with an East Lancs body, one of eight acquired from St Helens in 1958. Heading for Marsden Inn, it is being closely followed by No 242, a Karrier W with a Roe utility body. The 'Slow' sign provides a period piece of street furniture, of a type that is no longer seen today, whilst the railway semaphore signal is also of interest.

Trolleybuses always had to approach low bridges cautiously to give the trolley poles chance to adjust their angle to what, at times, was an almost horizontal position. In this instance, on 14 April 1963, South Shields

No 264 approaches slowly, the tight clearance being evident. It will be noted that the wiring is fixed in channels beneath the bridge. The trolleybus is a 1950 Sunbeam F4 with a Northern Coach Builders body.

Left: The 'Gay Hostess' double-decker coaches of Ribble and its wholly-owned subsidiary, W. C. Standerwick, caught the public's imagination when they were introduced on the Blackpool—London express service on 31 May 1960. The first to be received had represented the operator when Ernest Marples (then Minister of Transport) had opened the second section of the M1 motorway to Crick, Northants, on 2 November 1959.

Standerwick No 35 is seen at London's Victoria Coach Station on 6 May 1963. It was one of 12 delivered in 1961 and followed a batch of 10 that had entered service the previous year. Like all the 'Gay Hostesses', it was based on a Leyland Atlantean PDR1/1 chassis and powered by Leyland's 150bhp O.680 engine. Air suspension was originally fitted to the front wheels but was later removed. The 8ft-wide, 50-seat highbridge body, built by MCW, incorporated reclining seats, individual reading lights, a public address system and a toilet compartment. Initially, refreshments had been served by uniformed hostesses.

Above: The Teesside Railless Traction Board started, as its name implied, by operating trolleybuses rather than trams, its first vehicles running in 1919. It was also unique in that it was in joint ownership, with Eston UDC owning two thirds and Middlesbrough Corporation the remaining one third. It covered a small area to the east of Middlesbrough and went against the general trend of the 1960s by opening two route extensions during the decade. The last one, opened on 31 March 1968, was also the last trolleybus extension to be opened in the UK.

No 10, a 1945 Sunbeam W that had been rebodied by Roe in 1962, was photographed at Normanby on 14 June 1964. The system closed on 4 April 1971.

Above: Finishing its turning manœuvre around the central island at Normanby on 14 June 1964 is Teesside No 13 (CPY 311), a 1945 Sunbeam W with a Roe body dating from 1961. This was a heavily built-up area, so typical of the environs through which so many trolleybus routes ran. A number of local shops set the scene at the terminus.

Right: Trent Motor Traction's No 701 was an AEC Regent III, fitted with a Crossley synchromesh gearbox (Crossley had been taken over by AEC in 1948). One of only 10 delivered in 1950, it had an 8ft-wide Willowbrook body and was a handsome vehicle. Photographed in Nottingham on 28 September 1963, it was to be withdrawn a few months later.

Above: Leyland's Royal Tiger PSU1/17 chassis (**p**assenger, **s**ingle-deck, **u**nderfloor-engined) was produced for the Leyland single-deck bus body. This was solidly built and well finished, although the design was functional rather than stylish, having a very high waist-rail and a flat roof.

An example in Trent's fleet, No 351 dating from 1952, was photographed at Derby on 12 October 1963. In the background are No 1233 (CRC 833), a 1951 Leyland Titan PD2/12 with a Leyland body, and No 468 (68 ACH) a 1962 Leyland Atlantean PDR1/1.

Right: Withdrawn vehicles always have a sad appearance about them, and none more so than these United Automobile Services Bristol L5G buses, seen in central Newcastle on 15 April 1963. The general air of decline is heightened by the slave tyres, lack of destination blinds and the dust visible on the bonnets. A large number of these, with standard Tilling-style Eastern Coach Works 35-seat bodywork, had been put in service in the period 1947-50. All carried fleetnumbers prefixed 'BG' (**B**ristol, **G**ardner); from left to right are Nos 274, 186, 300 and 294.

69

Above: Seen in Newcastle on 15 April 1963, United Automobile's No BUE535 was one of a number of Bristol MW6G dual-purpose buses delivered in 1959/60. The designation 'BUE' stood for **B**ristol, **u**nderfloor (engine), **e**xpress. The Eastern Coach Works body was painted in the unusual but attractive livery that had been used by Orange Bros, an independent operator taken over by United in the 1930s.

Right: West Bridgford was an independently-administered (Urban District Council) suburb of Nottingham, lying to the south of the River Trent and running its own bus services. There were never many such operations; West Bridgford's was the first to commence, in 1914, and continued until 1968 when it was taken over by Nottingham City Transport.

The West Bridgford fleet was always immaculate, and a good example of this care and attention can be seen in ENN 700, a 1938 AEC Regent I with a 56-seat Park Royal body. The classic colour scheme suits the bodywork well, whilst the advertisement is hand-painted. The bus was photographed in the Old Market Square, Nottingham, on 2 July 1963.

Left: In 1963 West Bridgford required one double-deck bus as a replacement for another taken out of service after an accident. The replacement came in the shape of ACP 421, a 1947 AEC Regent III with a 60-seat Park Royal body, formerly No 47 in the Halifax Corporation fleet. Only recently acquired when photographed on 13 May 1963, it looked resplendent in its new colour scheme as it stood in central Nottingham. The size of both the letters and the numerals used in the destination blind is impressive.

Above: Whieldon's Green Bus Service was based in the northeast corner of Staffordshire, providing services in an area not adequately covered by any major operator, although its routes served places that were frequented by Midland Red, Potteries and Trent.

The locally-produced Guy marque was favoured; whilst some new vehicles were bought, there were also second-hand acquisitions, one of which was No 36, formerly Southampton Corporation No 101. This Guy Arab II, with a Gardner 6LW engine and Park Royal body, dated from the immediate postwar era and had worked for Southampton until the summer of 1962. It was parked outside the Green Bus depot, at Rugeley, on 25 August 1963. The company was taken over by Midland Red in 1973.

Above: This 1946 AEC Regent II with Northern Counties body was a long way from its original operating area when seen at Hythe, Hampshire, on 18 May 1964. Originally Western SMT No 311, it had finished its stage-carriage duties at Dumfries in the spring of 1961. A home-made door had been fitted to the rear platform to enable it to be locked up in its new role as a contractor's bus.

Right: AEC's postwar Regal I was produced in 1946/7, during which short time approximately 1,500 were built. It utilised the same engine, radiator,

gearbox, brakes, front wings and bonnet as the Regent II, and its basic simplicity, reliability and ease of maintenance ensured its popularity with operators.

Trent Motor Traction ran a large number. This example, No 746, with a Willowbrook body, was sold at the end of 1961 and converted for use as patient transport by a Cheshire home, most of the seats being removed to allow for wheelchair use. Named 'Crusader', it was seen at Staunton Harold Hall, on the Leicestershire/Derbyshire border, on 31 May 1964.

Red & White Services Ltd operated mainly in Monmouthshire and South Wales, but services ran to Gloucester and the Forest of Dean. Its interests also included Cheltenham District and Newbury & District, plus an operation at Stroud, but after the group sold out to the British Transport Commission in 1950 these passed to the appropriate former Tilling companies. The group was an inveterate user of Albion buses, and many were supplied in the years immediately following World War 2. Albion offered complete vehicles with Pickering bodies which, unfortunately, had short lives, resulting in many being rebodied in the early 1950s. One such was GWO 865, a 1948 Albion Valkyrie CX13 with a Lydney body, which, upon withdrawal by Red & White in early 1961, was bought by Contract Bus Services. It was photographed in an industrial landscape in Rotherham, Yorkshire, on 5 August 1963.

The Albion Venturer double-deck chassis never sold in such large numbers as its single-deck counterpart, the Valkyrie. The chassis was also sufficiently different to be classed as non-standard by the major bodybuilders, thus leaving the way open for smaller companies, such as Welsh Metal Industries, which bodied this example. The all-metal bodies were manufactured in Caerphilly and were sometimes built to a rather austere design, almost akin to a wartime utility. FWO 626 was a 1940s CX19, originally No L148 in the Red & White fleet, that had been withdrawn in the early months of 1959. It was seen in Nottingham on 14 July 1963, in use with Simmons & Hawker Ltd of Feltham, Middlesex.

Below: During World War 2 only one design of new single-deck bus was authorised for construction, this being the Bedford OWB. Derived from the recently introduced OB model, it was powered by a 3.5-litre, six-cylinder petrol engine that developed 28hp. The 32-seat utility body design was produced by Duple, and, although Mulliner, Roe and SMT also built some bodies, they all worked from Duple's design. Introduced in January 1942, the OWB was manufactured until September 1945 when production reverted to the OB. By the end of this period more than 3,300 had been built, mainly for the home market but with some for export.

During the 1950s and '60s many OWBs were bought by contractors for staff transport. One such example was PCH 175 (a registration issued in 1959), seen in the colours of Ford & Weston at Staunton Harold Hall, on the Leicestershire/Derbyshire border, on 31 May 1964.

Right: CET 442 was a Bristol L5G, one of a number delivered to Rotherham in the period 1938-42. Numbered 159, it had been rebodied in the late 1940s by Bruce of Cardiff (the body frames having been supplied by East Lancs), and at the same time the opportunity was taken to fit the later PV2 radiator. It had returned to its former haunts in Rotherham on 5 August 1963, in the subsequent ownership of Contract Bus Services. This fleet was run from Hereford Street, Sheffield, by T. D. Alexander, who also had a Scottish operation.

Below right: Birmingham City Transport's standard double-deck body was regarded by many as a design classic. The 54-seat examples seen here were built by MCW on Daimler CVA6 chassis. Originally Birmingham Nos 1482 and 1486, they were part of a batch of 75, delivered in 1947. Birmingham always had a reputation for running a well-maintained fleet, and any subsequent owner of one of its buses was always assured of a very sound vehicle. Elkes Biscuits, of Uttoxeter, Staffs, bought these for use as staff transport in the spring of 1963. They were seen at Whieldon's Green Bus depot, at Rugeley, on 25 August 1963, surrounded by miscellaneous withdrawn vehicles.

Leyland's Titan TD5 model came onto the market from the summer of 1937 and was a natural progression from the successful TD4. This one had been delivered in 1939 to Southdown as its No 250, and had been rebodied in 1949 by Park Royal. There was always a ready market for former Southdown vehicles, and this one was owned by Field Aircraft Services of Derby, being seen in Nottingham on 19 July 1963.